Tiller North

Also by Rosa Lane

Roots and Reckonings

Tiller North

Poems | Rosa Lane

to Sarah —

thank you for all of your
care and support —

Warmest, love 3·20·2016

SIXTEEN RIVERS
PRESS

Published by Sixteen Rivers Press
P.O. Box 640663
San Francisco, CA 94164-0063
www.sixteenrivers.org

ISBN: 978-1-939639-09-7
Library of Congress Control Number: 2015-948262

Cover and interior design: Josef Beery
Cover art: *Vespers,* Arlene Loesche Branick, acrylic on canvas
Author photo: Marilea C. Tanner-Linne

Three excerpts (16 lines) from "Lessons" from *New and Collected Poems: 1931–2001*
by Czeslaw Milosz. Copyright © 1988, 1991, 1995, 2001 by Czeslaw Milosz
Royalties, Inc. Reprinted by permission of HarperCollins Publishers.

"Fish Eyes," from *Roots and Reckonings* by Rosa Lane (copyright © 1980 by Rosa
Lane), is reprinted by permission of Granite Press, East.

CONTENTS

III

FOREWORD

Tiller North ends with the word *sing,* a final act in a volume of poems that narrates sorrows and pays tribute to the Maine people Rosa Lane comes from. She offers scenes looked over carefully, as everyone takes their place at the table. She tells of making it through a sense of unbelonging, imprinted by rejection based on class and cut-off dreams mitigated by fierce love, hard work, and constant relation to family, place, and the rules of the season.

Her lyric touch brings the air alive, and she makes everyday hungers and hopes shine visible, often as scars. But she sings into them and hears the music there, harsh and tender, as any wound speaking its power. Rosa Lane's poems read as if they have been at her fingertips and written themselves into being, each carrying each closely, carefully remembered in body time and sung in a clear voice. She praises the steady hands of father, mother, grandparents, and great-grandparents. As the title suggests, the way to shore and survival are what counts in the stories here.

Everyone gone before has the last word, and it is these very same people who sang the poet into being. She understands this: her father, in particular, at the rudder of *Tiller North,* who flew her into a sky of wonder, is part crow and part hummingbird, both vulnerable and daring. He has given her the possibility of "stitching" blooms in the air and speaking from the crow's dark, shining throat.

There is necessity and there is also light in *Tiller North*—both are the day's long praise of the life recorded here.

—Beatrix Gates, author of *Dos* and *In the Open*

I

Since that moment when in a house with low eaves
A doctor from the town cut the navel-string
And pears dotted with white mildew
Reposed in their nests of luxuriant weeds,
I have been in the hands of humans.

—Czeslaw Milosz, from "Lessons"

BOATS NAMED WOMEN

Fishermen call them women:
Christina, Beulah, and the *Marie L.,*
chained to a piece of granite dropped
into the cove. Gutted hulls of wives,
daughters, granddaughters float
their curves, squint painted trims
through a foreground of dense fog,
pull lips against moorings of weather.

Sprocket, Chummy, Red Bickford, Tinker,
and my father haul around Thumb Cap Island,
their love wrapped in newspaper,
brought home, and laid on the washboard.

My father's feelings are simple: hover over
fillets, gather hunger beside the knife. At two
in the morning, she opens her blouse,
lays the sharp edge at the side of her breast:
Here, if that's all you want, take it.

JUNE BUGS

Electricity buzzes the yellow bulb
in Maine's humid heat. June bugs bomb
the porch light with spiny legs — date-colored
and oversized.
                Spring peepers pin the night,
pitch a universe in my mother's kitchen, except
I have not yet occurred to her. She is sixteen,
and I will be hers in less than a year.

Supper's on the table for the boy who will be
my father, his nineteen-year-old body big
and husky. He rinses dried splashes
of work from the day's ocean into a small
blue basin, enameled and filled
with hand-pumped water drawn from the well.

Fireflies light the field aflame. Conceived in the heat
of summer, I appear a small spark of night
planted in the deep crevice between them.

ARIA

At night my father and I build traps
in the shed: oak slats spaced the width
of a hammer head over three arched bows
of chokecherry, two five-pennies preset,
the dead-on pound. My father's lips pucker
a Camel, nails pinched to the side, his radio,
splattered with paint and bait,
set to Mozart and Wagner.
                                The branding iron
searing *P. Lane* into oak at honey-light
just before burnt dusk, he sings sundown.
The wolf arches his back, throws
his head to the stars, sings full timbre
The Marriage of Figaro, his cigarette
streaking the air red hot.
                                My mother
hates opera. She slams the door,
festers the kitchen over stew she says
will be better tomorrow. The ceiling
busy with insects, she leans against the stove
with one eye to the tube warming up *Gunsmoke,*
yells us to the table. My father peaks crescendo
in high tenor. Mother turns up the gunshots,
ladles stew into bowls. My father dances
to his captain's chair set at the head,
the whole table arrested, TV turned to snow.

TOMBOY'S TOGGLE TO LOVE

I was held hostage
by a tribe not mine,
age seven, alien. I knew this
then, exactly as I know it
now. I set the amber bottle
afloat in the North Atlantic,
where I slipped
my message: *Find me.*
If you are a woman,
I love you.
      I sang
my transistor's dial
set to Sinatra, the only call
to love I knew, transmitted
from the cove's edge.

All that summer, I listened
for return air waves, Morse codes
of arrival, any one of you
to come ashore. Instead,
      my mother's
      WGAN radio
dominated the broadcast, blasted
from her Protestant window,
overlooking my whole
irredeemable, irrevocable life.

AUNT HAZEL

Her dark hair, perfect
pin curls, lush lips — red
thick lipstick — fleshy legs
under the full-flowered skirt.
She was my girlfriend — no one
knew it.
        My five-year-old body
pulled by magnets, drawn
down on Nanny's
couch where Aunt Hazel
leaned into pillows, pulled me
against her, stroked
my long curls as Uncle Al
strummed the guitar
and made me sing

"You Belong to Me" right there
in front of everyone.

BAMBOO

I.

The first day I went into the clump,
it was with Pamp, when he made us flutes.

We stared at his knife's edge
as it slit the notch to make a mouth

and the tool that bored holes
for fingers to pinch notes

up and down. His bamboo patch
grew thicker each year

where the mailbox hung its rusty jaw
and could not talk. One summer

our arms wove our bodies
through the stalks to the center,

a canopy of leaves arced
green over our heads. Tinted

light dimmed us, spears of sun
shifted aim in the wind. Our clothes

whispered to the ground, our chests
pulled taut with tiny buds.

Hands on each other's shoulders,
we stood rubbing our smallnesses

against one another. How young
we were — so smooth, empty, and pithless.

2.
Once, we heard someone coming,
and Pamp's large face parted the flutes

of bamboo, found us: your body sucked
into a pinhole—the whole clump

a ribcage for your beating heart. Pants
bound at your ankles, you zigzagged

through the stalks. Me? Suspended,
I watched my body fold back into the crisp

bed of dead leaves — Pamp's mouth
a crack of anger, his bamboo stenciled

my skin — red branches. My lips
hummed closed, tight. That night

I could not sleep. From the upstairs
window, I looked down, watched bamboo

rustle night into dawn, the thick crown
of leaves trembling in the light August breeze.

Through the open window, I could hear
the squeaky jaw of the mailbox flap louder,

laughing and laughing out of its old rusty head.

POND

When the pond turns, Pamp said,
you smell fresh mud, a dank mist

floats above brackish water.
The first fifty degrees flush out

spring from the bottom of winter,
when frogs lay a handful of jelly

dotted with black eyes. The adolescent
girl wades thigh high into the pond

in her grandfather's hip boots,
scoops millions of embryos

into her glass jar. In the back shed
she watches tiny eyelet births explode

into swirling swarms of motherhood. She
chooses one, returns the rest to the pond,

watches metamorphosis in stages
of legs and shrinking tail.

The slippery head emerges
half-in, half-out of the dark liquid air.

Out of nowhere the neighborhood boy
swells a secret, a young groin of heat—

in the cool spring of April. He grows
amphibian into the palm of her hand.

She undresses a couplet of soft nipples,
salamander brown, and swims and swims

the farthest edges of her backyard.

DEER AND WOMEN

1.
Tonight, the moon is out watching
for deer and women. One eye
tacks the orchard, round
and full. A few leaves remain,
flick silver across the field—
warning. Frost: snaps of light,
cool diamonds harden the landscape.

The moon is out watching
for deer and women. I lie
in shadows and wait. I hear them,
a herd of eyes   couple
    and hold.
        They know
        I am here.
They pull me through the dark
with invisible threads. I want them
to know I am as wild and untouchable.

2.
Tinker said he knew everything
about deer and women. His eye
rests on the pasture fence, narrows
along a barrel of cold steel. Notching
the bead, he pins her across the field.
Black hooves tear open the air,

a brown rush disappears
into sprigs of green dark—
      spring-loaded,
      she falls.
      With a strike
of a match, Tinker lights a Lucky.
Sucked back, white ash grows
a ghost above his head, then vanishes.

She hangs from her hooves
in the apple tree. Against
the flow, blood drains
into her head, a full red chamber
where her black eyes float open, return
the girl's wild, unbroken stare.

3.
Winter is mostly melted.
I find a doe and fawn lying
in a woods clearing. Tufts of snow
fill small pockets
of understory. Bones imprint
cavities of April's mud. I pick up
their faces, hold them to the sun,
eyes blink holes of light.

I lean the deer against a tree, place
the pelvis in the fork of a stick, hang
their skulls on branches, stick
their legs into soil. I wrap
them in cloth, run them

through the spring field to my bedroom,
lay them in a box, skulls
nested one inside the other, legs
folded along the sides, nuggets
of spine piled in the corners,
and placed them under my bed,
where sleep suspends one eye open.

Tonight, the moon is out watching
for deer and women. The deer know
I am here. They pull me through the dark
with invisible threads.
                    They tell me:
Run a soft path, make no sound
where you go, brown-flash   run
as fast as you can, run untouchable, run.

SIRENS

I.

In spring, deer flies drive the cat's ears
crazy. The house itches inside
flakes of paint. Our father's fish shanty lowers
into the backfield early summer,
when morning glories raise walls
with sweet bursts of powder blue. A workbench
holds remnants of his underworld:
fall's spiced rope—*potwop* we call it—gnarled
in the corner, steeped in brine, braided
with seaweed and dried crabs.
                                    Then December's
dreaded turn, the vastness of survival
any moment could shatter,
like the winter when school closed,
when water in our eyes could have frozen,
settling gray light into sockets of ice.

2.

Headlights in January drop us off, sweep
our shadows across the snowfield,
the potbelly stove curls ghosts
above the peak. Our father's
red plaid body blurs behind a grid
of dimmed orange: the whole fish shanty
a beached creature, half buried, its scales
ragged shingles against slate blue.

The bell buoy clangs the harbor
with another storm warning—our father
already knows, his lips ajar with a cigarette,
his one note on exhale. New spits
of snow flicker the field. All winter
he builds traps stacked in a pyramid
where he ascends to sirens
who will call for him

come April.

ELEGY FOR A SNOWMAN

The torso rolls the whole yard
into a ball, gathers speed

down the path passing my mother's
clothesline hung heavy

with bedsheets blown open.
My mother has pinned my father

at the shoulders, his body frozen
in long johns. And earlier, how he wanted

to hold her light in his arms, melt
their early morning. Snowman's

belly imprinted with debris,
candy wrappers, bottle caps,

dirt from the driveway. My father
lights up, his head tilts

into the flame, and we look for eyes
that will sparkle in moonlight.

Base to torso, torso to head,
the snowman's breath turns raw-

carrot orange. And the dog
follows the man into March,

his piss punctures the base
pale yellow. He runs the perimeter

of the yard in a path rolled down
to last summer's grass.

Branched arms forked
with clumsy love,

purple cold. All winter we watch
the man melt and freeze, grow

more go-lucky, less care
with disappearing. Plaid cap, loose coat,

smoking corncob, rocks for ears
hear the lightness of early April's snow,

a line of pebbles for the mouth
speaks the last few syllables of winter.

BESSIE

My great-grandmother

Trees tattoo the room
with gray   cracking
an afternoon below zero.

The curve of evening
hunches over a bowl of broth
in front of kerosene heat.

Foot holes poke a path
in the snow. I bring her a few
groceries: bananas, bread,

butter. Walls record her life
on cold plaster; the black breath
of cigarettes hovers

under the eaves. Narratives
pimpled with Braille tell patterns
of history. She traces

my long, curly hair, which was hers
eighty-eight years ago. *Crows
stole my eyes*, she says.

That is when she knows me
by touch, when she sees me
with her fingers and calls my name.

WINTER CROWS

Morning
after last night's squall:
little holes of onyx
fly open,

a constellation of black stars
rises ragged just above
last October's field
        one by one.

A tremolo of notes lands
on wires, one measure
of argument, operatic
and raw, one staff of need,
one cleft of desire:
        caw, caw, caw

they call for my father who told us
one day in the car, shifting
octaves of distance, pointing up,
        One day I will be
        one of them.

II

From them I received the names of plants and birds,
I lived in their country that was not too barren,
Not too cultivated, with a field, a meadow,
And water in a boat moored behind a shed.

— Czeslaw Milosz, from "Lessons"

OMEN

A wreck of weeds washes up pale
sea glass at the deck's edge.
Wild blooms scribble across the back-
field, then skim the top fringes
of meadow, afloat in this freak summer
we could not fathom at first.

June began with our father's boat
pocked with barnacles, laid keel up,
overturned by a cancer undetected, then
the rash of salmon that appeared
in a sunset across his chest and brooded
in his lungs that hung on a plastic line —
a pump of oxygen constantly not enough.

The three of us: sunflowers planted
around his bed, our heads tracking
every move of our father's fall. Windows
pull to the east, each morning
a golden ratio of the day before.
His face half-hidden under the wing
of his arm, his body disappearing,
his future sliding back just ahead of us.

APOGEE

The day after his fourth chemo, our father
sold his lobster boat to a young man,

laid the money on the counter, then
mowed the neighbor's lawn for a couple bucks.

We kept eye on the bob
of his shiny bald head   afloat

above the chokecherries and the blades
that spun him across the yard

of an afternoon, his confidence restored
along cut edges of grass. For a moment

we turned away, set the table
for tea, when we saw the tractor reel

against the birdhouse post. One arm
hooked to the mast, he stood

on the tractor's seat, one free hand, thick fingers
poked back the nest as delicate as he imagined

a mother made it. He knelt, pinched up
three babies fallen in tufts of straw—still beating life

behind gray lids, wrinkles of yellow beak
oversized and hungry—rearranged them

one by one as if their mother might not notice.
But this fourth one, a small flit, no more

than a knuckle of life, lay limp in the crease
of our father's double palms. Broken,

weeps slip high-pitched from the taut tube
of his throat, compressed

in his hands stained with accident and nicotine
sucked to places too late to change, he

turned to his daughters — gulps of air
heaving inside his canister chest —

this marksman, who once boasted of trophies,
twelve-point bucks and bear, he confesses his life

to this minuscule feathered face wedged
between thumb and forefinger, arrested

head to head, eyes, windows of heaven
open against the sea of clover, yarrow,

and mustard brushed in meridians of light,
his boat floated back around the side

of the house, the piece the young man
could never buy. In it, our father drifted away,

the flick of bird pecking his path ahead,
retracing everything he had taken,

better than whole again.

SIGNALS

We scuffed a road map of days,
maybe weeks, with signposts
    and signals we did not recognize.

We relied on our father, at the heart
of the room, to tell us where we were.
    We did not know, since he was busy

dying. His barrel shape sheeted,
his fingernails clubbed
    and yellow. One thing for sure,

he was moving to a different
country. We watched him accept this
    without question. He finished

his business, packed his suitcase with
a few things: hunting rifle, dog, cigarettes.
    On Thanksgiving,

I took my turn on watch, dozed
to the hiss and pump of his breathing.
    I did not know this would be his last night

home. He thrashed awake, his legs
running a fast bicycle under the sheet.
    My father in my arms: *Run, fly me.*

He climbed onto my waist. Held,
we whispered a flight over treetops. He locked
    eyes with my mother; a volume of life poured

between them. First responders maneuvered
his gurney over a furniture of firs, above the kitchen table
    of an ocean, around appliances in the house he built

on a dirt road mapped twelve miles into early winter.

THRESHOLD

Tonight, light snow lifts an aura
from the landscape. My father's
moon, mathematical, rises
and pulls tides beneath the ice, groans
past late December's dusk.
      My father's head
washes up on the pillow, his skin
glinting hospital heat, the neck
of the cold river bronchial and narrowing.
The hiss of his chest snarled in knots
along a taut tinsel of oxygen. He is
no longer talking to us on the hoarse
side where more and more nothingness
gathers about his bed.
      Right in front
of us, he floats out
to the Damariscotta River, tidal
and glacial, at the shore of spruce fir,
the phosphorous blurred edge
      all we have left
      just before the cold green line
      flattens his lungs, freezes him shut.

FATHER

My father stitches the backyard. I say
my father because my mother knows

my father has returned as a hummingbird.

I say *stitches* because the hummingbird
threads blooms bush to bush, his needle

beak basting stamens housed within skirts
of petals, mending rips of difference.

That last night, his daughters sat in a circle
puckered tight to his bed. I was one of them.

We tended each small flicker of life
left. How could we survive without him?

He had already begun to hover
            above us. I know now
what he was thinking:

> *If they could only admire*
> *my new ruby throat, my*
> *emerald green pulse suspended,*
> *my beating wings few ever see.*

This moment was complicated.

Our mother bloomed open against hospital white.
She saw her daughters: rearranged patterns of him,
            perennial and timeless.

With each daughter's face in her hands,
she let us go for the first time.

                              That night,
three birds of paradise flew up-stem
            into a sky he left us   to fly into.

MOTHER

January 2003

The sunroom drifts a snow globe
into the chop of a blizzard. A candle
blinks our mother's face on and off
along the coast. She navigates
a galaxy, stars ping
her glass helmet.
                             She returns
to her helm just off the kitchen,
leans over the table, sets a bowl
and cup across from hers. A little
gust of wind animates the curtain.
She knows he has landed his orb, arrived
with the snow, hungry for dinner.

WINTER'S KITCHEN

The boiler, copper and oval,
straddled two burner plates, and a poke
of flames coiled in a wick
lit a snake that lived
in the old cookstove,
hidden, blue and yellow. The air
of our small Maine house,
soaked with kerosene, sucked down
a tubular throat from an orange jug
of poor-man's heat. Mornings glazed
with night ice, the cold waist-high,
we skated from our beds across a pond
of green leafage and cracked roses,
where spring lay dormant somewhere
beneath the pumpkin-backed linoleum.

Every day was cleaning day. Back
and forth our mother dipped scalded
water from the copper boiler
to the wringer washing machine,
sloshing its white belly in a dance
of cleanliness. Slabs of clothes fell
into set tubs galvanized on her hip,
clipped to the frozen wind
of the clothesline.
                        At dusk, she
carried our whole family
into the house, zero-degree wind

at her back. This is how she said
she loved us: bras frozen solid, white
cones strapped in her arms, she placed
our small breasts in front
of the fire. She cradled my father
in his long johns, board-stiff,
checked him for stains up to the light,
stretched him across the counter. She
melted us limp into folds of cotton. Her love
for us lay in puddles of winter on the floor.

RECKONING

For seventy-seven years,
my mother and her mother
have barely spoken. I could be
either one of them: I am
she who gave up her child. I am
also the child left. I am
the child who was a mother
to my mother, a child
who was never a child, you know,
the way generations
repeat themselves.

The scene I want is this.
Alchemist tools sit on a table:
crucible, retort, mortar, pestle.
The alchemist grinds trace elements:
a bruised landscape, a past
chilled by a swipe
of shadow   blued
back behind a yellow
porch glow, filaments twisting
light against the wall.
                              That night
my mother's mother packed her suitcase
with a few things, slipped from the house,
walked along a short moonlit path
in a hurry, knocked on the neighbor's door,
handed away her daughter's two years,

disappeared where the road narrows
at the reach in 1934.
For seventy-seven years,
no matter how much time passes,
it remains 1934.

This is
when the alchemist transforms one thing
into another, when it could just as well
have been the reverse, and maybe instead
that night a mother held her child close
against her body, fled past
the neighbor's house that blended
into her dark as she pulled a blanket tight
around them all these very same years.

FALL

Above the coast, trees have already turned their heads
from summer green to full-dress golds, reds,

and browns. Branches cock and wait for winter. Boats
sleeved in white wrap cradle their hulls in cocoons,

a seasonal stage of metamorphosis at the marina,
every last bit of farm canned, dried, or frozen in dirt cellars.

The Atlantic reaches her fingers up ragged inlets as if land
were torn from a deep blue book along which I will drive

the rental. My mother, alone now, uses my arrival to cook.
The smell of ham hock opens the door, the table set for two.

She waits for thirty-three hundred miles to disappear
between us. We sit and eat. She says, *Another winter*

with no lights four houses each way. She points
to the Pomeranian: *All I have left is him.* She bends over the sink,

stares into the yard, afraid she will disappear unnoticed,
like the cold that stole her flowers, spring sealed in a pod.

III

Their lessons met, it is true, with a barrier
Deep in myself and my will was dark,
Not very compliant with their intents or mine.
Others, whom I did not know or knew only by name,
Were pacing in me and I, terrified,
Heard, in myself, locked creaky rooms
That one should not peep into through a keyhole.

—Czeslaw Milosz, from "Lessons"

TILLER NORTH

Take Route 130 nine miles
where it dead-ends at the coastal tip,

keep your eye on the spire,
how it peaks above ragged pines

torn from a small length of ocean:
shingled shacks drunk with fog,

the mouth of John's River, a bar
of khaki sand, a stand of piers rusted

in salty air, Dora's cow pasture blurred
with brutes down meadow. How the fog

dampens fisher boats wedged at the wharf,
arched glass stained with light on the hill.

~

Households begin at the Point,
where fisher boys drive

their cars fast to the cliff,
test their brakes, scare

their girls, who squeal and dive
for safety into dangerous

arms. Tongues of the bell buoy
bang a rhythm of ocean in backseats,

when sixteen-year-old bellies grow
pregnant, birth armloads that suck

tiny breasts, unready. The young stumble
along a path of church bells calling them

to kneel Protestant pews and swallow
white wafers of a single mind.

~

Fisher boats named women wait in the cove,
anchor lines tied at the nose, nets piled

in the hold. Our father stands there waving
across the salt air, our mother at the shore

squinting the sun, seaweed floating
her black hair across the surface ahead

of winter already moving in. The three of us
run to the school bus each morning.

Our father's fingers, cracked with cold, count
singles laid on the kitchen table at night,

our porch lights lit proof of survival at the edge
of the harbor we are damned to leave.

HOW WE WERE MADE

1.

Bullies pinch our arms with paper claws, their cootie catchers pass
imaginary germs, hiss us to backseats on the yellow Blue Bird.

The school bus noses through town, its windows snapping scenes:
Hanna's Garage, Reilly's store, the Munsey House. Howard's

school bus gears up Snowball Hill past Mr. Frank's General. Winter
sun blinds the eastern shore. Wind badgers trees along Huddle Road.

School will be an eternity, fourth grade at the room's back—
the three of us, Clarion, Robert, and me, placed there

                                        as if absent.

2.

It seems now unbelievable how differences would obstruct light,
light embodied by the very star by which the day's sky is made

equal—and outside it, how we were made less
            visible. How ordinary hopelessness became. Even now,
            how easily we stop just short of the dark, then in it.

MAROONED

The hovel burns red with fall
where poverty smokes. A tangled colony

of cousins, each kid born a burden,

bandages of dusk
wrap gauze around nights

of dimmed futures. Not a one
had a damn chance to dream,

marooned on the west side of town.
I was one of them, born mixed,

stained with stigma:
>Never amount to much.
>Indians know nothing,
>no money, can't get out.

Like one cousin, who went crazy
with unbearable otherness. He's in the asylum

now, so my mother says. He stands
at his window, watches a constellation

of fireflies: little pieces of spark
against a backdrop of stars

about the same size hovering the dark field
light years away. Fireflies?

Stars? He weighs this question
with not one ounce of care

which is which.

BINGO

Lucy's shack sat on cinder blocks
pressed into peat near the bog,
a piece of real estate
no one wanted. Saturday night
down at the hall,
she laid navy beans
on numbers, played six cards,
won a few coins
on the left straight.
                           She drives
headlights up the throat of driveway
pounded hard by the last rain. Trees
crawl across the face
of the house. Her porch light
burns a small hole at the door.
Her boyfriend can't wait up,
he said—her daughter's silhouette
in the upper window riding horseback
on a horse she never sees.

NEIGHBORS

Small strands of color braided fall uphill,
air frigid with argument. We overheard
each syllable unravel, sudden, furious.

The whole thing seemed wound
in one hand talking. The mouth
of the index finger loud and clear.
His throat pointed out each decibel
of betrayal, an arrangement
red-faced and genetic. Again,

dogs barked alarm across the valley,
but not one of us thought different,
except this time, past Thanksgiving,
he snapped off her head as quick
as a bloom from its stem.
          At the back
of the house, the gun left half
his face in the oak-brown leaves
where he was found crawling yards away
by the dog he loved,
          his sons
          following
exactly this same half-headed path.

NANNY AND PAMP

The paddock compressed
into bales: sweet honeysuckle,
vetch, clover—the whole loft
eaten down through winter. Great-
grandmother readied her horses
to pull the buckboard to Hope,
to bring her daughter, Flora, fourteen,
from upcountry to coast, raised
remote by kin: horse whisperers.

Great-grandmother and her sons
slatted reins along the trail hoofed
and watered by springs. Her boys
cupped grain and sliced apples
to horse lips to meet a sister
they did not know.
                              The sky
trotted ahead to beat sundown —
two days, one night each way.
A farmer let them sleep in his barn,
water their horses.

When the buckboard drew back
onto Huddle Road, Pamp grabbed Nanny
off the wagon, so she told.
                              At fifteen,
Nanny birthed the first baby,
born blue; thirteen followed: one

for General Patton, one
for the Battle of Normandy, one
for electronics, two to pneumonia,
and a few for fishing—my father,
one of them, born in the middle
on a couch beside a pan of warm water.

Her kitchen: checkered tablecloth,
lunch of cold toast, skillet of lard,
curly thread from something red
on the treadle. Her hands clicking
a string of arthritic knots in doilies
crocheted for birthdays, she sat below
her children in black and whites
patched in a quilted collage behind
the smoky glass frame hung on the wall.

She wore three flowered dresses
one over the other, rotated
through washtubs, dried on alders
to the south.
     Pamp had bad spells,
mean as an unruly brook some time
around April. I was their grandchild,
had Pamp's long arms,
but never meant to be much
since I was a girl with curly hair
down my back, the kind men wanted,
Pamp said.
     I used his hip
boots, waded their pond, boiled sap

on their stove, slept in the upstairs
bedroom above the cove's inlet.
Their language became mine:
pot burner, stove poke, washboard,
wringers.

                       After Pamp died
in his sleep, from the hollow
of her wood-armed chair
after ninety-one years Nanny
couldn't think of one single thing
to say beyond each birth of her babies.
Her geraniums, spiced and pungent
in pots, lined the sill. Even in winter
bursts of scarlet bled her room
to the outside, tinted the snow.

PAINTER

Simon was Burton Blaisdell's brother, lived
across New Harbor Road in a house found

at the end of a footpath, softened behind
summer's green veil of oaks and maples,

fractured in a layer of winter's branches.
Windows, gray pieces of light, stared back

at cars. We craned our heads to catch him,
the hermit: caked clothes, a navy beret

gone black, hair self-scissored and capped
white under a bowl. He placed Pemaquid

on canvas: the Atlantic crashes against
his mornings, jars of brushes, oils in muted

blue-greens, white chop rolls onto his beach,
whole days spent on one wave. Fish boats pull up

to the easel, yellow skins, suspendered, bend
over the haul. He ties the starboard

to Gilbert's wharf, empties a catch of silver
flipping harbor lights against salmon-blended

dusk, brushes night into winter's village sleep.

FISH EYES

Gulls circle
barrels of herring. Near
Thumb Cap, my father
levers the *Marie L.* neutral,
gaffs the buoy, spins potwop,
pulls trap to starboard,
threads herring onto the needle
slid through sockets strung
into the pot's head,
one trap after another.

By afternoon, fish eyes roll
on the floor of the boat,
look up. I look down
at the waves, pick up
the eyes, handfuls,
toss them overboard
behind me into the wake. I see
them roll through the salt —
marbles of light   blinking.

THE SHED

1.

Inside, the dark hummed,
and a panic of roses
climbed the outside walls: thorns
spiked small footholds upward
along the gray shingles. Roses
burst their heads open, small tongues
peeled back from the center.
A quick pulse of blood, red moments
here, and then, petal by petal, gone.

2.

The roof barely peaked above
the bushes, walls leaned away
from weather. Forbidden, the door
slanted back. I was five
and moved about the shed
every day, watching. Tools,
worktable, fishing nets, wild cats
hovering, their eyes, yellow thumbtacks
pressed into walls of dark, watching mice
staple themselves into corners closer
and closer for a catch.
                    Spiders spun
my legs and arms up the ladder to the loft,
wrapped in silk. Dry pine walls crawled
with insects running shiny beads

of oil into crevices. One knee jacked
weight up and over. Blades of sun
pierced the wall, the whole shed
scraped clean. A salted fish hinged open,
hung by its mouth from a nail
in the doorway. A two-fingered hand
reached in, ripped fish off the bone, mouthfuls,
leaving a fish-shadow pointed upward,
swimming forever to the surface
along the back wall.

3.

Uncle Walt's hand frightened me. Once
he made me touch it: a row
of stubs. *Bang, bang, bang,*
bullets took them, one by one,
the First World War. I pictured
their perfect shape   lying
somewhere foreign. I pictured
them probing and clawing earth
from the other side, wiggling
root-like and stubborn homeward,
moving toward him, deliberate,
making their own fisted cave to rest in
at night.

        Perhaps
I heard them then, clicking in weeds
next to the shed, fingers
snapping. Or perhaps

his fingers flew half-wing
through air. Or they were white
and crawled only in winter along snow,
or even the fingers lie now
beside each other like empty husks,
insides turned to dust,
blown to a hillside where flowers bud
and flare up once each year.

4.
He grabbed his tools, hoe,
the five-pronged digger, trowel and claw,
hitched his one bad hip
to the garden. I watched him kneel
and inch along a row of new carrots,
thinning and pulling them
from their resistant sockets. His thumb
and forefinger drew circles
around the ones untouched. I could see
piles of carrots lying cross-boned
in the path behind him. I stared
as if he might pull his fingers
from the garden, or find them
in the snap beans rattling bones, pods
hanging beneath green heart-shaped leaves.

5.
From the other loft window, I saw
his wife step out from the house
and reach into the roses

up to her elbows, snipping stems.
How the flowers bled in her arms,
her nose deep into the petals,
pink shadows on her neck.

      At night
how his two fingers must have brushed
the hair from her face. In bed,
those moments when her mouth
opened deep like the roses. I can see
those lost fingers tapping
and tapping at the window.
How the fingers must have watched
their absence touching her.
How she took his two-fingered hand
in hers, pressed the stubs to her lips,
kissed the blood back
to each one again and again.

HURRICANE

Hideous how one second changes fact:
that terrible day in November

when Kennedy was shot. And Gert's roller rink,
same day, teetered on rocks at Little Brown Beach,
went down in a hurricane, washed into the Atlantic.

How flawed this way of it.

For decades the rink stood there in repose,
above a smooth bed of whiskey sand,

where the moon swirled its drink and posts waded
knee deep, the salted breath of seaweed

damp and sour. Below its floor at low tide,
babies were conceived at intermissions.

News broke. The black and white Zenith flickered
our living room with Dallas, the limousine rolling

across the wall, the crack of gunshots, an insanity
of bullets buried in the mind of the hurricane

raging the coast that day,
its intent to take everything.

How momentary. How disturbed. That night,
I went to the attic where my skates
rolled out of the box,

met Gert there
who waited and watched me skate

the air above Little Brown Beach until I saw her

push from shore, wave from her roof peak,
grow distance to a speck. The moon

brought back a few split timbers.
Her grid of posts remains stunned

as if they still cannot believe what happened.

BARN WHISPERER

Once a hub of horses, the three-story barn leans
ten inches toward the field, teeters

on rotted hemlock
and stones half-toppled. The whole weight

draws into one small corner of a stall,
wracked and stitched in angled light, strands

spun in rotted dark. Planks scarred by hooves,
glazed with dung, the peak — a cathedral of bats —

blesses the night. Lofts each side elevate
decades of pasture, sweet August harvest,

filled with labor and hay, rolls of our love
tossed into the crib of winter. Bridles

still hang on a hook. Posts rubbed smooth,
honey-colored and chaffed with oils from necks

and chins, ears and manes. The barn wants to lie down,
grieves for gravity. The barn whisperer listens,

rearranges the foundation with thoughts, chinks,
and shims, lifts the barn, jack and pulley,

puts it to rest for a week to concede.
Posts and beams sing dissonant, untwist

and strain, mortises and tenons adjoin, tines of tension.
The barn speaks to the whisperer as if they sit

across a table eye-to-eye in conversation or argument.
The whisperer lifts one edge of the eave,

hushes secrets into the barn's ear
as would any lover—the barn made as true

as the snort of its ghost horse
lying there   now resting.   See it?

DESERTED HOUSE

1.
The gray horse disappeared
in shadows pooled

at the edge of the house. A woman
in the doorway watched dust

from the truck settle back into the road,
her hand over her mouth, the screen

diffusing the lines of her body
as a ghost. The plum tree

in the yard ripened cheeks
indigo below her eyes.

He stepped out of the truck,
entered the house, slapped

the door closed
against them.

2.
Years later, this house sits quiet. I walk
around it, my hands cup eyes

inside each attached shed: voices,
broken bones, bare thistles,

dried horse hooves hanging
in the barn. Above

the weeds, irises
extend their purple palms, spreading

fingers. I reach for them. They hold
the face of the house in their hands.

THE HUNTER

Wails of the hunter's loon
reach across the pond, its cry
echoing inside us. We float in mist
at margins of a lower meadow.

We grew like weeds
on the other side of town, unwanted,
troublesome. The ones we troubled
shucked us like ears of corn
held up to the light, examined
for disposable grist or usable ware.

Our mother swirled our bodies
each night in tubs, enameled,
stove-heated water   tempered
by buckets of hand-pumped cold.
She wrapped us in cotton, cut
our hair by kerosene light—
clipped and groomed as clean
as she imagined us to be one of them,
to fit in somehow, to blend.

~

I didn't realize how much of me
was not mine, how much I earned
myself back. I filled myself
with a quiet stash as one would fill a jar

with seed. In it, I held my future, a handful
of jacks thrown across the floor,
the sweep of asterisks into the hand
on the one bounce I was given
by the rich man from New York, the man
my father took fishing afternoons
after a day's haul as his father had done
years before. This rich man from New York
handed me a constellation of stars
of another world
where I relearned to live.

                                  I once said
I would not look back, but in poems I do. I hunt
for the cry of the loon. And when I find it,
I know, for me, I am living.

MAINE SUMMER

Late July afternoon, cicadas tune the air, high-pitched grasses
brush the details of a Wyeth painting, egg tempera: the hunter

at *Turkey Pond* down in the swale of *Christina's World* made
alive here on Barren Hill where I return these weeks. This day

filled with repairs on the 1768 farmhouse: hand-hewn
timbers, king pine boards, and cellar stones stacked

by revolutionary men. Old canned beans, carrots, and pears
stock their shelves, and corn is still in the horse crib. I pace

their pumpkin pine floors. Air ripples near the old birthing
room where pilgrim women snipped and rinsed babies

into the world. A knock at the door, no one there,
but the old crow at the top of a spruce caws a beat,

which tells me my father is near. I drive three miles
past the summer people to the horizon where parallels

of the universe meet along a thin line of air, where
all not here live whole again, like Wyeth's Christina,

who no longer drags her body with her elbows up the front
field, but walks, polio-free, a footpath to the farmhouse.

She invites me in. We sit at the table that belongs to both of us.
We share tea and sip from the same lips that belong to both of us.

We merge on the rim of a cup tucked centuries ago into the pocket
of the barn wall — handle out, placed by the hand that lived there —

an interval of time   the cicadas every seventeen years

                                                    sing.

ACKNOWLEDGMENTS

Grateful acknowledgment is made to the following publications, in which these poems were published, sometimes in earlier versions: *The Briar Cliff Review:* "Apogee"; *California Quarterly:* "Winter Crows" and "Mother"; *Crab Orchard Review:* "Threshold"; *New Millennium Writings:* "Father"; *New South:* "Deer and Women"; *Ploughshares:* "June Bugs"; *Roots and Reckonings* (Granite Press, East): "Fish Eyes."

My gratitude also goes to Jeanne Emmons, poetry editor of *The Briar Cliff Review,* for selecting "Apogee" as the winning poem for the 18th Annual First Place Award; to Alex Williams-Carr for selecting "Father" for the First Place Award of the 38th New Millennium Prize for Poetry; to Brian Oliu, who selected "Deer and Women" for second place for the 2014 *New South* Writing Contest; and to Cornelius Eady, who also selected "Deer and Women" as National Runner-Up for the 2013 Cape Cod Cultural Center's Poetry Competition.

I am especially honored and grateful to have worked with the following extraordinary poets and friends whose micro/macro lenses provided exceptional insight and invaluable feedback crucial in the making of *Tiller North:* Jeffrey Levine; Sharon Coleman; my Green Hearts Collective writing group; the members of Sixteen Rivers Press, especially Lynne Knight, Carolyn Miller, and Terry Ehret; Bob and Ann Morrill, native Mainers, who kept me true to my roots; and finally my partner, Catherine, who accompanied me in and out of every detail with deepest care and support.

Sixteen Rivers Press is a shared-work, nonprofit poetry collective
dedicated to providing an alternative publishing avenue for
San Francisco Bay Area poets. Founded in 1999 by seven writers,
the press is named for the sixteen rivers that flow into San Francisco Bay.

SAN JOAQUIN • FRESNO • CHOWCHILLA • MERCED • TUOLUMNE
STANISLAUS • CALAVERAS • BEAR • MOKELUMNE • COSUMNES
AMERICAN • YUBA • FEATHER • SACRAMENTO • NAPA • PETALUMA